CLOTH I

NERINA ROBERT

CLOTH DOLLS

NERINA ROBERTS

δελος

CAPE TOWN

Contents

Delos, 40 Heerengracht, Cape Town

Photography by Nato Barnard
Illustrations by Jenni Jewels
Produced and designed by Wim Reinders & Assoc. cc
Cover design by Abie and Jasmine Fakier
Set in 11/13 pt. Palatino by McManus Bros (Pty.) Ltd. Cape
Town
Printed and bound by National Book Printers, Goodwood,
Cape

First edition 1989

ISBN 1-86826-063-1

Introduction

Seven of the most adorable cloth dolls ever. Yours to make and enjoy. Designed to be loved by adults and children alike.

This book not only shares knowledge and expertise acquired after years of doll-making, but also carefully teaches, step by step, the art of obtaining really professional results.

The patterns for the dolls and their clothes are full-size and the instructions are detailed and precise so that both the novice and the experienced doll-maker will find the making of the dolls a pleasure.

A section is devoted to the making of the accessories which are so important. The correct shoes for the outfit, a catty, some silkworms or a doll stand, are all ideal finishing touches.

Allow yourself the pleasure of participating in this wonderfully creative hobby. Awaken some nostalgic memories of childhood, apply your own ideas and let your imagination run free or simply make dolls for the fun of it. There is a ready market for well-made cloth dolls.

Description of the dolls

KIRSTEN

Kirsten is 70 cm tall and because of her size and beautiful clothes has been designed mainly as a display doll. She is unsculptured and her limbs are sewn on. Her lovely curls are made from ordinary wool which is baked in the oven.

SIMON

Simon is 62 cm tall and quick to make. Partially sculptured and with a wig that takes only minutes to make from nylon fur. Dressed only in T-shirt and jeans, Simon is fully jointed and suitable for both play or display.

ANNABEL

Annabel is 56 cm tall and is every little girl's favourite. Fully jointed and with lots of sculpturing detail. Annabel's clothes are specially designed for easy removal by young children.

JEWEL   FRANKIE

Both are 50 cm tall and full of character. Fully jointed and with lots of sculpturing detail.

KIMBERLEY

TANDI

Both are 40 cm tall. Adorable bend-legged babies with lots of sculpturing detail and fully jointed. May be posed lying, sitting unsupported or crawling. Quick and cheap to make, the babies are definite best-sellers.

1 Equipment and materials

Fortunately, embarking on a hobby of cloth doll-making does not require much initial outlay as most of us already have the basic equipment and materials.

A SEWING MACHINE

Although modern sewing machines are a treat to work with, especially when making a doll's clothes, they certainly are not essential and the simplest machine will do.

It is, however, essential to ensure that the machine is in good working order before you begin, as

not only should the stitches be strong and neat, but you will experience great difficulty in sewing the finer details such as the neck curves, fingers and ears, if the machine is faulty.

Skipped stitches are the main cause of distress.

As the dolls have been designed to be made from a stretch fabric it is advisable to use a blue ball needle in the machine. These needles are readily available at sewing shops and are designed so that the ball point enters between the fibres of the fabric without cutting them and thus causing possible runs. Change your needle, after sewing about three dolls. Do not wait until it breaks. The average needle is dulled beyond repair after about 10 000 stitches and an average medium-sized doll with single seams has between 2 000 and 3 000 stitches. Synthetic fabrics will dull the needle even sooner. Remember to change back to a normal needle for the clothes.

BODY FABRIC

The dolls are designed in cotton knit, and for the best results it is essential to use the specified fabric. Buy a good quality material with a minimum amount of stretch going across the fabric from selvedge to selvedge. If possible, choose, a fabric where both sides may be used as the right side as this will help tremendously when making left and right legs and arms. Be absolutely sure that the fabric will not run when punctured with a sculpture needle. Colour is also very important and should be chosen with care. Experiment with dyes if you feel adventurous, or stay with soft peach for the white dolls and rich shades of brown for the coloured and black dolls.

THREAD

Machine thread, as well as very strong thread such as a twist or upholstery thread for stringing the doll and for the sculpture work.

STUFFING

Always use a good quality acrylic stuffing to ensure that the doll has a smooth finish, is light and washable. Foam chips and cut-up pantihose are totally unsuitable.

AIR-SOLUBLE PEN

Obtainable from sewing shops. This pen is used to draw on the fabric and the marks will disappear after a few hours or on the application of water.

SCULPTURE NEEDLE

The needle should be at least 10 cm long and is used when stringing the dolls and for sculpturing.

COVERED SHANK BUTTONS

Four for each doll, about 30 mm in diameter. These are used for jointing the doll so that the arms and legs will move freely and the doll will sit unsupported.

SMALL STICK

A selection of small sticks, chopsticks or crochet hooks, to push the stuffing into tiny areas such as the fingers and toes.

FABRIC PAINTS

Most fabric paints will do, but for realistic eyes it is better to use a fairly liquid paint and a 00 or 000 brush.

NYLON FUR/WOOL

Long-pile nylon fur or chunky wool is used for the hair.

SHOES

Felt, vinyl, feather leather or suede are suitable for the shoes.

DOLL'S CLOTHES

A well-stocked sewing basket and plenty of oddments of pretty fabric, lace, ribbons, etc., should be sufficient for the making of the clothes. The exact requirements have not been listed.

2 Preparing the pattern and cutting out the dolls

The patterns are all actual size. Trace the patterns on to a firm cardboard, transferring all the details. Cardboard is used as it will prolong the life of the traced pattern and it is easy to draw around. Cut out all the pieces and punch a small hole in each. After use, the pattern may be threaded on to a pipe-cleaner for safe storage (Diagram A). Select all the pieces to make the doll of your choice.

Large dolls like Kirsten, Annabel and Simon will require 50 cm of fabric, 150 cm wide.

Double the body fabric with the selvedges together, and place on a cutting board or table. Place the cardboard pattern in position ensuring that all the arrows go in the correct direction (Diagram B). Beware of turning one or more pieces incorrectly in order to fit the material (Diagram C). This may result in the doll having one short fat arm and one long thin arm, or the clothes may not fit.

Draw around each piece with an air-soluble pen. Remove the cardboard and return the pattern pieces to the pipe-cleaner.

Carefully cut out all the pieces of the doll *except* the arms and the ears. These are easier to sew before cutting out and at this stage are cut out roughly.

DIAGRAM A

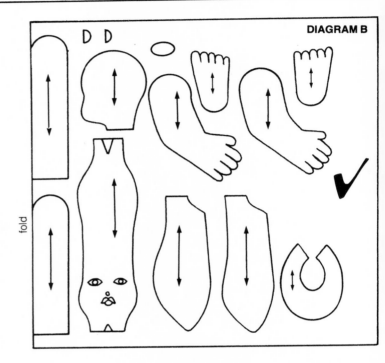

DIAGRAM B

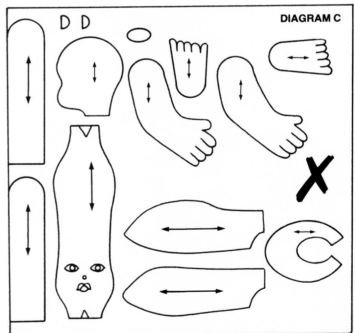

DIAGRAM C

3 Painting the face

If you are an experienced artist you may wish to leave the painting of the face until the doll has been completed. In this way you will ensure that the features are in exactly the correct position, and you will also have the opportunity of selecting features to suit the way the doll has turned out. For the less talented, now is the time to try your hand at painting. If your first attempt is not successful you will only have wasted a small portion of fabric. Try again and again, if necessary. Painting beautiful faces takes practice but is well worth the effort. You may, of course, embroider the faces if you prefer.

Use liquid paint but be sure to shake the bottle well and often or you may find that the paint will become thin and could "bleed" into the fabric. Buy a few good-quality brushes in sizes 00 and 000. Needless to say, these should always be kept scrupulously clean.

THE EYES

(All dolls)

Be patient. Always allow each coat of paint to dry before applying the next one.

1 Trace the position of the eyes on to the centre head panel.
2 Paint the whole eye area white. Allow to dry and apply the second coat.
3 Trace the iris again if necessary, and paint the iris area the colour of your choice, but not too dark.
4 Paint the pupil area black and add a tiny white highlight.
5 Using a 00 brush and a darker shade of your chosen iris colour, paint tiny radiating lines all around the iris. Add a few black lines as well. Outline the iris in the darker shade or black.
6 Using a 000 brush, outline the entire eye in black, making the upper line darker and thicker than the lower line.
7 Begin at the corner of the eye when painting the lashes. Draw the paint up in a slight curve to a fine point. Try to do each lash in a single stroke (Diagram D).
8 Paint the brow in a shallow curve (Diagram E). It often helps to turn the doll upside down when painting the second brow. Try to use a colour to match the hair or brown. Black is very severe.

THE MOUTH

Mouths are easier to paint but the colour is important. Never use plain red. Try to find a salmon colour or add a little white to tone the red down to a pinkish colour.

1 Trace the position of the mouth on to the centre head panel.
2 Following the diagrams and the colours indicated, paint the mouth of your choice (Diagram F).

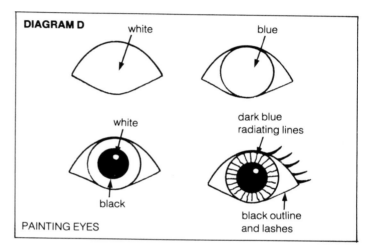

DIAGRAM D — white, blue, white, dark blue radiating lines, black, black outline and lashes. PAINTING EYES

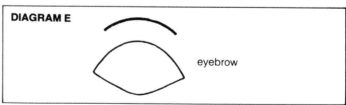

DIAGRAM E — eyebrow

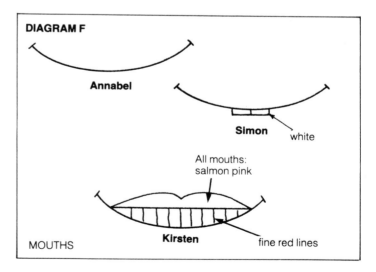

DIAGRAM F — Annabel, Simon, white, All mouths: salmon pink, Kirsten, fine red lines. MOUTHS

4 The sewing

Cloth dolls need to be well sewn as a lot of stress is placed on the seams during the stuffing and, if they are designed for play, the dolls will have to endure rough handling.

It is advisable to sew the dolls by machine, but if you are forced to hand-sew, then it is essential to use a backstitch and very strong thread.

Skipped stitches are caused by a build-up of lint around the bobbin. Perhaps the tension needs adjusting or the thread is incorrect for the needle.

Use a stretch or small zigzag stitch for sewing all the seams. If your machine does not have this, use an ordinary straight stitch but sew all the seams twice. An average-sized stitch will be fine but a smaller stitch should be used around the small curves such as fingers and toes.

All dolls are sewn in the same way unless otherwise stated. Use 4 mm seams throughout.

THE HEAD
1 Sew the chin dart and the centre back of the head dart in the centre head panel.
2 Sew around the ears on the line leaving the – – – side open. Cut out. Turn to the right side and sew on the solid line. Pin the ears to the **head sides**, facing forward, and machine sew. Fold the ears back and secure with a small hand-stitch (Diagram G).
3 Pin and sew the centre head panel to the head sides **A** and **B**.

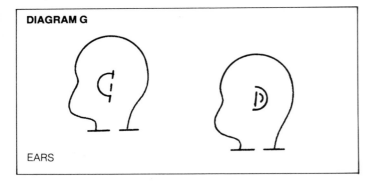

DIAGRAM G

EARS

THE BODY
1 Sew the centre back and then the centre front seams for all dolls except Kirsten. Sew the shoulder and the side seams, leaving the bottom open as indicated for the stuffing.

2 Have the body on the WRONG side and the head on the RIGHT side. Place the head inside the body at the neck, right sides together. Match the chin dart to the body centre front seam and the back of the head dart to the body centre back seams. Kirsten does not have a centre back or front seam on her body so extra care must be taken to ensure that the head is in the correct position. Pin and sew around the neck. Turn to the right side (Diagram H).

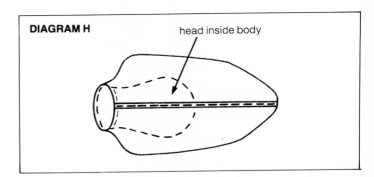

DIAGRAM H — head inside body

THE ARMS
If you cut out the arms you may find it difficult to get neat fingers. Imagine trying to pin those tiny fingertips together and then still having to sew them without the machine sucking the fabric in. *Try this method.*
1 Cut out the arms roughly.
2 Change to a see-through foot on the machine to enable you to see the line at all times. Sew on the line, changing to a smaller stitch when you get to the finger curves. Sew one or two stitches, leave the needle in the fabric, lift the foot and turn the work slightly, lower the foot and do one or two more stitches. Repeat until the fingers are done. This takes a little extra time but is well worth the effort.
3 Sew all around the arms *on the line*, leaving the tops open, as indicated, for the stuffing. Cut out and turn to the right side. Sew in the finger-dividing lines (Diagram J).
4 Now cut out the arms. Turn to the right side and sew in the finger-dividing lines (Diagram J).

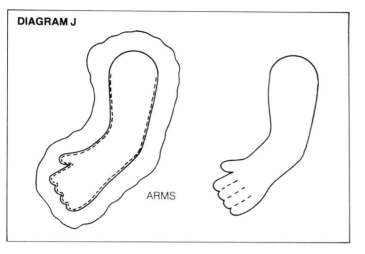

DIAGRAM J

ARMS

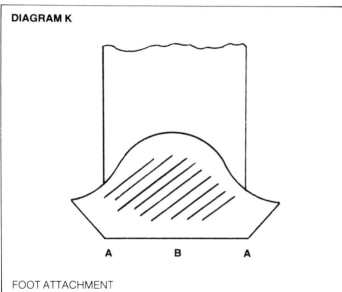

DIAGRAM K

A   B   A

FOOT ATTACHMENT

THE LEGS

Kirsten, Annabel, Jewel, Frankie and Simon

1 Sew the upper feet to the lower legs matching **A** to **B** to **A**. (Diagram K).

Sew the back seams of the legs, matching **C** to **A** to **D**. Leave the tops open as indicated for stuffing. Kirsten does not have toes. Sew on the soles. Cut away excess fabric, if any, and turn to the right sides.

2 The remaining dolls have toes, and an easy way to ensure that you will have a left and a right foot is to proceed as follows:

a Redraw the outline of the soles and the curves of the toes if they are not absolutely clear. Remember to reverse one.

b Place the feet side by side with the big toes together and with the drawing side nearest the table.

c Carefully place the upper feet over the soles and pin.

d Now sew *on the line* all around the soles and the toe curves. Cut away the excess fabric and turn to the right sides.

e Sew in the toe-dividing lines.

Kimberley and Tandi

Sew the back seams from **A** to **B** and then the front seams from **C** to **D**. Leave the tops open, as indicated, for stuffing.

Sew on the soles. Cut away any excess fabric and turn to the right side. The toes will be sculptured later.

5 Stuffing the dolls

Correct stuffing is probably the most important part of doll-making. No matter how beautiful the costume or how artistically the face is painted, an incorrectly stuffed doll will never look right. The golden rule is to ensure that the dolls are stuffed *hard*. Large dolls such as Kirsten, Annabel and Simon, should take at least about 700 g of stuffing each.

HEAD/BODY

Begin by stuffing the head and body. Use *large* pieces of stuffing and feed the stuffing into the head. Using your hands, push the stuffing up against the crown of the head. Continue feeding the stuffing into the head until it is hard. Remember that you are working with a stretch fabric, and it is very important that you do not allow the head to become bigger and bigger. Squeeze, mould and pat the head at all times while you work to ensure that the stuffing is compacted and the head retains a good shape. Continue in this manner until the body is also firmly stuffed. The neck should have no wobble whatsoever, but it is also important not to overstuff the neck or it will be too fat and the clothes will not fit. Try compacting the stuffing by strangling the doll. Sounds terrible, but it works like a charm. If this does not prove successful, then a small stick may be inserted into the head/neck/body area during the stuffing. Sew the body closed, using ladder stitch (Diagram L).

THE ARMS

Using a small stick, push tiny pieces of stuffing into each finger. Use two or three pieces per finger. Continue stuffing the arms, once again squeezing to compact the stuffing. When the arms are full, insert a cover button down into each arm about 2 cm from the top on the side which is to be against the body. From the outside place a pin through the shank to hold the button in position. Turn in the raw edge and sew the arms closed, using ladder stitch (Diagram M).

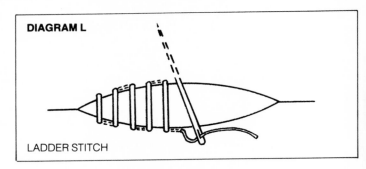

DIAGRAM L

LADDER STITCH

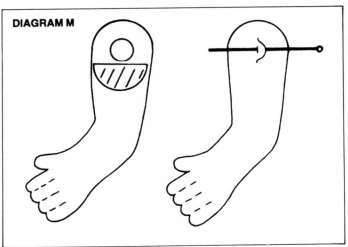

DIAGRAM M

THE LEGS

Stuff the feet firmly, using a small stick to push the stuffing in the toes. Pound the feet on the table or the palm of your hand to keep the soles flat. Continue stuffing the legs, using large pieces of stuffing, squeezing and pulling them as you work to retain a good shape. Roll small "golf" balls of stuffing in the palm of your hand. With the aid of a stick or knitting needle push the balls into the knee area of the legs of Kirsten, Annabel, Jewel and Frankie. (The knees will be sculptured later.)

Insert the buttons as for the arms, and sew the legs closed, using ladder stitch and folding in the raw edges at the same time.

N.B. Kirsten's arms and legs are not jointed and therefore do not require the insertion of buttons. Sew closed.

6 Stringing the dolls

1 Place the arms against the sides of the doll so that the tops of the arms are level with the shoulders.
2 Using an air-soluble pen, make a dot on either side of the body at the place where the shank of the button touches the body. (The dot on the pattern is an approximate indication only, as it may not be in exactly the correct position once the doll has been stuffed.)
3 Repeat for the legs, placing them in a position that looks right and keeping them very low on the body, or your doll will have large hips. Mark on the dots as for the arms.
4 Use a long needle and 3 metres of very strong thread. Double the thread before threading the needle and, gathering all four threads together, tie a large knot at the end.
5 Leave a tail of thread. (This tail will be used to tie a knot later.) Put the needle through the shank of the button. Enter the body at the dot **G** on the left side. Go right through the body and bring the needle out at the opposite dot on the right-hand side.
6 Pick up the right arm through the shank of the button. Enter the body again near the dot **G** at the right side of the body and go right through the doll again, bringing the needle out near dot **G** on the left-hand side of the doll.
7 Squeeze both arms tightly against the sides of the body and knot the threads (the tail left in the beginning and the thread in the needle). Cut off the excess thread (Diagram N).

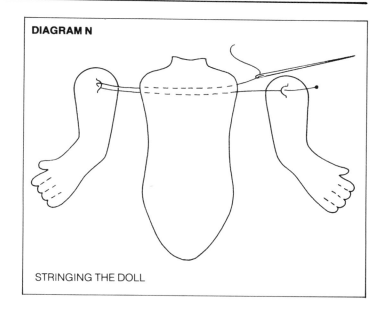

DIAGRAM N

STRINGING THE DOLL

8 The legs are done in the same way but using dots (H). Legs are more difficult to do and often a second or third attempt is necessary.
9 **Kirsten:** Hand-sew the arms and the legs to the body where indicated. The arms hang down her sides with the thumbs facing forward. Ensure that the feet also face forward.

TEST
If the stringing is correct the arms and legs will stay in the position in which they are placed and not fall back down. The doll will also be able to sit unsupported.

7 : Sculpturing the face and body

Sculpturing will only be successful if the doll has been firmly stuffed. Even then it may still be necessary to push a needle about 2 cm or 3 cm into the doll, and to lift more stuffing into the area to be sculptured, e.g. the cheeks, buttocks, etc. The shape of the doll depends on where the little stitches are placed and how tightly the thread is drawn up. As each artist works differently, no two dolls are ever quite the same. This is what makes it such an exciting project. Try it. It takes a little practice but is well worth the effort. Always use a strong thread doubled and a long sculpture needle. If this is your first try. Good luck.

———— Thread on the outside
------ Thread on the inside

CHUBBY CHEEKS

All dolls

1 Enter at **A** at the neck and exit at the inner corner of the eye. Making a tiny stitch, re-enter at the inner corner of the eye and return to **A**. Pull firmly on the thread to draw up the cheek.
2 Making another tiny stitch, re-enter at **A** on the neck, but this time exit at the outer corner of the eye. Making a tiny stitch, re-enter at the outer corner of the eye and exit at **A** at the neck. Pull firmly on the thread (not too tight) and fasten off.
3 Do the other eye in the same way.
4. Put powder blusher on the cheeks (Diagram P).

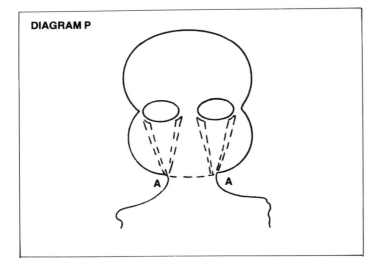

DIAGRAM P

THE NOSE

All dolls

1 Gather all around the nose (Diagram R).
2 Put a small piece of stuffing into the centre and pull up the gathers tightly to form a small ball. Fasten off but do not break off the thread.
3 Squeeze the nose to look like Diagram R1. Wind the thread tightly around one side of the nose (Diagram R2) to form a nostril, and then around the other side (Diagram R3) to form a second nostril.
4 Fasten off and ladder. Stitch the nose to the face.

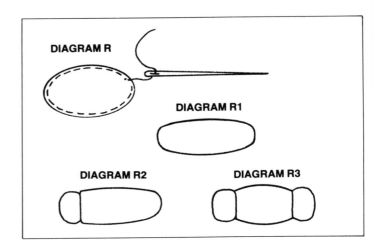

DIAGRAM R

DIAGRAM R1

DIAGRAM R2

DIAGRAM R3

THE MOUTH

Jewel and Kimberley

1 Before you begin sculpturing the mouth, insert a needle and lift the stuffing into the upper lip area.
2 Enter behind the nose and exit at the corner of the mouth **X**. Making a tiny stitch, re-enter at the same corner **X** and return to behind the nose. Pull tight. Enter again behind the nose and exit at the opposite corner of the mouth **Y**. Making a tiny stitch, re-enter at the same corner **Y** and return to behind the nose. Pull tight. If necessary, insert a needle again into the upper lip area and lift the stuffing. Re-enter behind the nose and exit at **X**. With the thread on the *outside*, enter at **Z** and exit behind the nose. Pull tight. Re-enter behind the nose and exit at **Y**. With the thread on the *outside*, enter at **Z** and exit behind the nose. Pull tight. The upper lip has now been formed.

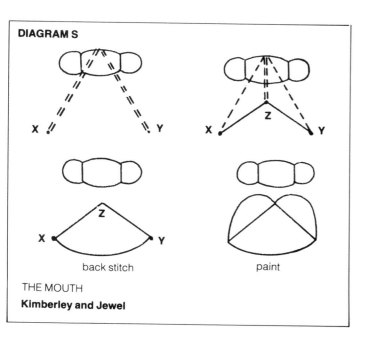

back stitch   paint

THE MOUTH

Kimberley and Jewel

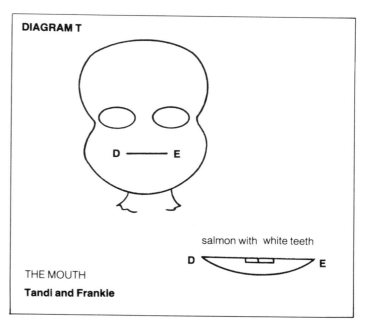

salmon with white teeth

THE MOUTH

Tandi and Frankie

3 Make the lower lip by sewing a semicircle of backstitch from **X** to **Y**.

4 Paint the outline of the lips, using brown paint for Jewel and pink for Kimberley. The inside of the mouth is coloured with blusher (Diagram S).

Frankie and Tandi

1 Enter at **C** at the back of the head. Go right through the head and exit at **D** at the corner of the mouth. With the thread on the *outside*, enter again at the opposite corner of the mouth **E** and come out again at **C**.

2 Pull firmly on the thread and fasten off (Diagram T).

3 Paint Frankie's mouth according to the instructions on the diagram.

Annabel

1 Paint the mouth according to the instructions on Diagram F.

2 Place a dimple at each corner of the mouth. Enter behind the ear and exit at the corner of the mouth. Make a tiny stitch and return to behind the ear. Pull tight and fasten off.

3 Do the other corner in the same way.

Kirsten and Simon

1 Paint the mouth according to the instructions on Diagram F.

2 Dimples as for Annabel may be added.

KNEES AND ELBOWS

1 Enter at the dot on the knee/elbow and exit at the opposite dot.

2 Squeeze the knee/elbow gently and sew backwards and forwards between the dots until the knee/elbow "holds" (always with the thread on the inside). The elbow will be complete but you may wish to continue with the knee as follows:

3 Enter at the lower dot on the front of the knee (leave a tail of thread hanging) (Diagram U). Exit at **P** on the side seam. Take thread across the back of the leg on the *outside* and enter at **Q** on the opposite side seam. Exit at the lower knee dot.

4 Using the tail you left at the start and the thread in the needle, pull tight and tie off. Loose the threads.

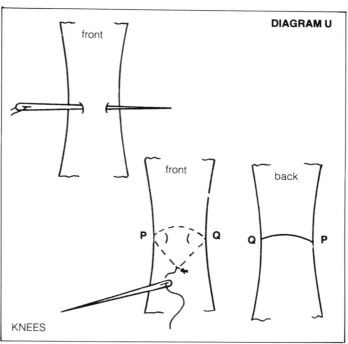

DIAGRAM U

front

front   back

KNEES

WRISTS

1 Make a tiny stitch at **F** on the inner arm. With the thread on the *outside*, go across the wrist and make a tiny stitch at **G**.
2 Still with the thread on the outside, go back to **F**.
3 Pull firmly on the thread and fasten off (Diagram V).

NAVEL

1 Make a row of gathering stitches all around the navel (Diagram W).
2 Pull up tightly, pushing the interior of the navel in with your finger or a pencil.
3 Fasten off.

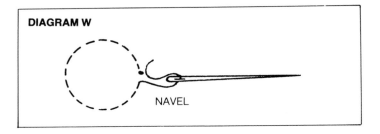

NIPPLES

1 Make a row of gathering stitches all around the nipple (Diagram X).
2 Pull up tightly and allow the interior to protrude.
3 Fasten off.
4 Paint pink using blusher.

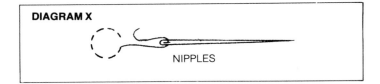

BUTTOCKS

1 Make a large neat knot at the end of a *long* double thread.
2 Enter at the navel and go right through the doll. Exit at the upper buttocks dot (Diagram Y).

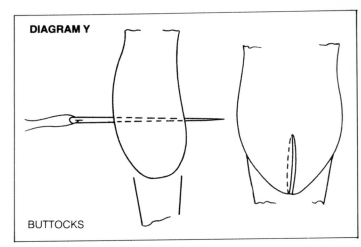

3 With the thread on the *outside* to form the dividing line of the buttocks, enter at the lower buttocks dot and exit at the upper buttocks dot. Draw up the thread firmly. Repeat.
4 Fasten off.

TOES

Kimberley and Tandi

1 Enter at **A** on the sole of the foot and exit at **A** on the top of the foot (Diagram Z). Bring the thread over the toe tip and again enter at **A** on the sole, but this time exit at **B** on the top of the foot. Pull tight. One toe has been formed.
2 Continue in this manner until all toes have been formed.
3 Fasten off.

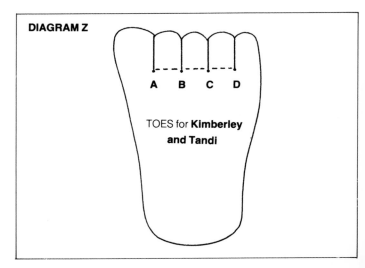

8 The hair

WIGS MADE FROM NYLON CRAFT FUR

Simon, Frankie, Tandi and Kimberley

1 Draw a circle on the back of the fur fabric. House-hold objects such as plates and bowls are useful to draw around. The approximate diameters should be:

Simon	22 cm
Frankie	20 cm
Tandi and Kimberley	18 cm

2 Cut out the circle, taking great care not to cut the pile.
3 Place the fur on to the doll's head with the right side against the head, and pin small darts all a-round until the fur fits the head like a cap.
4 Sew in the darts and cut away the excess fabric (Diagram hair 1).
5 Sew the wig to the doll's head, and brush and trim where desired.

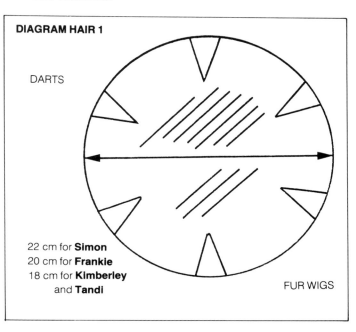

DIAGRAM HAIR 1

DARTS

22 cm for **Simon**
20 cm for **Frankie**
18 cm for **Kimberley** and **Tandi**

FUR WIGS

CHUNKY WOOL CURLS

Kirsten and Jewel

You will need lots of 4 mm knitting needles or blue wire cut into 50 cm lengths. It is nice to have about 50 rods but far fewer will do provided you are pre-pared to bake the curls in batches.

1 Secure the wool at one end of the rod. Wind the wool tightly around the rod until entirely covered. Tie off. Continue until 100 g has been used for Jewel and 200 g for Kirsten.

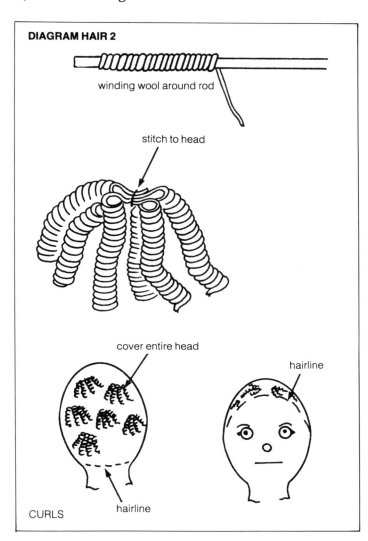

DIAGRAM HAIR 2

winding wool around rod

stitch to head

cover entire head

hairline

hairline

CURLS

2 Wet the wool thoroughly.
3 Bake in a moderate oven, about 120 °C, for 30 mins. Switch off and allow to cool in the oven.
4 Slide the curls off the rods and cut into desired lengths, e.g. 15 cm for Kirsten and 6 cm for Jewel.
5 Hand-sew small bunches of curls as securely as possible all over until the entire head is covered. Jewel's hair must be cut very short, and will look even more realistic if the wool is unravelled. Kirsten's hair may be left long (Diagram hair 2).

CHUNKY WOOL PONYTAILS

Annabel

1 Cut a piece of cardboard 50 cm x 24 cm and a piece of tape 24 cm long.
2 Wind 100 g thick wool lengthwise around the cardboard, packing the strands close together.
3 Put the tape across the centre of the cardboard/wool and hand-sew to hold in place.
4 Now cut the loops at each end and remove the cardboard.
5 The hair may now be securely machine-stitched to the tape.
6 Put the hair tape-side down on to the doll's head so that the machine-stitching forms the centre parting.
7 Hand-stitch the hair to the head all along the centre parting.
8 Lift half the hair and apply glue to the whole side of the head. Gently lower the strands, a few at a time, on to the glued area, directing them towards point **X** where the ponytails will tie. Repeat for the other side.
9 Tie the ponytails first with wool and then with the ribbon bows (Diagram hair 3).

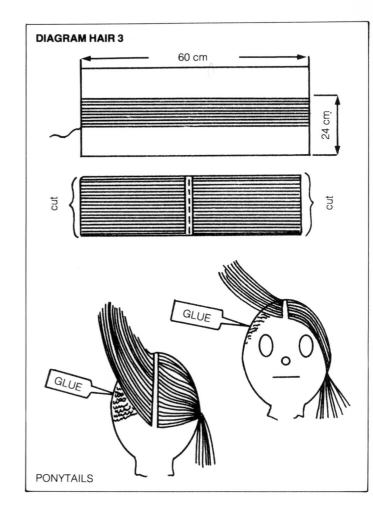

DIAGRAM HAIR 3

60 cm

24 cm

cut

cut

GLUE

GLUE

PONYTAILS

9 Instructions for making the clothes

4 mm seams have been allowed.

N.B. It may be necessary to adjust the patterns for the clothes slightly, as cloth dolls differ in size depending on how they are stuffed and the type of fabric used for the body. All the basic instructions are given for the assembling of the clothes, although some of the trimmings of the garments have been left for you to choose.

THE DRESSES

Kirsten, Annabel and Jewel

1 Trim the front of the bodice as desired.
2 Sew the front and the backs of the bodice together at the shoulders.
3 Fold and press the back opening. Hem. Make the buttonholes and sew on the buttons. Press-studs may be used (Diagram clothes 1).

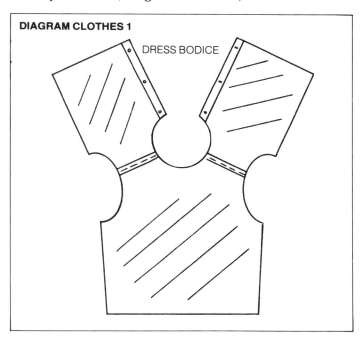

DIAGRAM CLOTHES 1
DRESS BODICE

4 **Kirsten only:** the neck frill. Cut a strip of matching fabric about 40 cm x 5 cm. Hem the two short sides. Hem the lower edge of the frill and trim with lace. Gather the upper edge of the frill to fit the neck and tack into place.
5 Cut a strip of matching fabric and bind the neck of the dresses for all dolls.

6 Make a narow hem at the lower edge of the sleeves and trim. Stretch and sew elastic to gather the lower edge of the sleeves about 3 cm from the bottom.
7 Gather the curved edge of the sleeve to fit the armholes. Tack and sew. Sew the sleeve seams and the side seams of the bodice.
8 Trim the skirt as you please.
9 Hem the bottom and the sides (back opening).
10 The smocking at the waist of Jewel's dress is optional. Gather the top of the skirt to fit the bodice. Tack and sew (Diagram clothes 2).

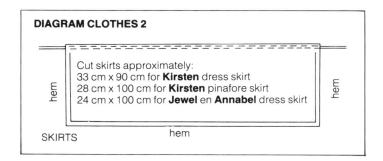

DIAGRAM CLOTHES 2

Cut skirts approximately:
33 cm x 90 cm for **Kirsten** dress skirt
28 cm x 100 cm for **Kirsten** pinafore skirt
24 cm x 100 cm for **Jewel** en **Annabel** dress skirt

hem   SKIRTS   hem

THE PINAFORE

Kirsten

1 Sew the shoulder seams of the bodice. Sew the shoulder seams of the lining (Diagram clothes 3).

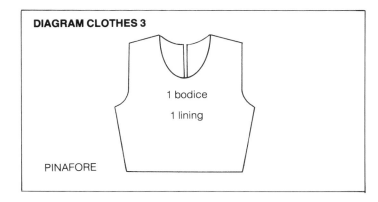

DIAGRAM CLOTHES 3

1 bodice
1 lining

PINAFORE

2 Sew the bodice and the lining together around the neck and down the back opening. Press. (Diagram clothes 4).
3 Hem the curved edge of the sleeve frills and trim with lace.

23

DIAGRAM CLOTHES 4

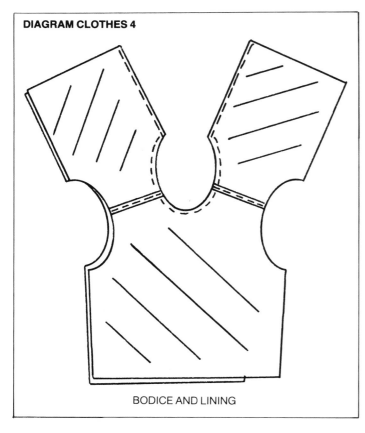

BODICE AND LINING

DIAGRAM CLOTHES 5

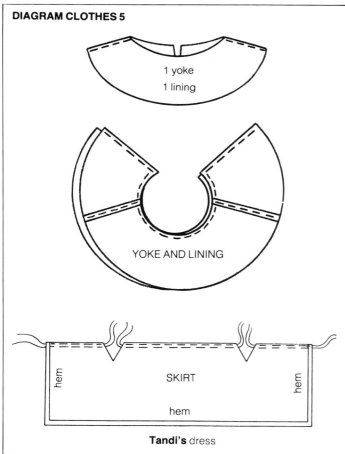

1 yoke
1 lining

YOKE AND LINING

hem   SKIRT   hem

hem

Tandi's dress

4 Gather the straight edge to fit the armholes. Tack and sew.
5 Sew the underarm and side seams of the bodice.
6 Trim the tops of the pockets and sew into position on the skirt.
7 Trim the skirt as desired, adding lace, ribbons and pin-tucks.
8 Hem the bottom and the sides (back opening).
9 Gather the top of the skirt to fit the bodice. Tack and sew (Diagram clothes 2).

THE DRESS

Tandi

1 Sew the shoulder seams of the yoke. Sew the shoulder seams of the lining.
2 Sew the yoke and the lining together around the neck and down the back opening. Turn and press.
3 Fold and press narrow hems at the lower edge of the yoke and the lining. Tack lace to the very edge of the yoke.
4 Hem the lower edge of the dress and trim with lace. Hem the back opening and the underarm armholes.
5 Gather the front and the two back sections of the dress so that they fit the yoke between the large dots.
6 Place the gathered skirt between the yoke and the lining, tack and topstitch.
7 Add two press studs to the back opening.

T-SHIRTS

Simon and Frankie

Approximate lengths of rib trim before folding.

Simon	1 piece 22 cm x 4 cm for the neck
	2 pieces 18 cm x 4 cm for the sleeves
Frankie	1 piece 21 cm x 4 cm for the neck
	2 pieces 14 cm x 4 cm for the sleeves

1 Sew the shoulder seams.
2 **Frankie:** Bind the lower sleeves with rib trim. Gather the tops of the sleeves slightly to fit the armholes and sew. Sew the sleeves and side seams.
3 **Simon:** Bind the armholes with rib trim. Sew the side seams.
4 Ensure that the shirts will go over the dolls' heads. If not, hollow out the necks a little more. Bind the necks with the rib trim.
5 Hem the bottom of the shirts.

THE HAT

Tandi

1 Cut the crown of the hat, using a small plate approximately 24 cm in diameter.
2 Iron on vilene to stiffen the brim of the hat (optional).
3 Sew the short side of the brim to form a circle. Repeat for the lining.
4 Tack lace to the edge of the brim. Place the brim and the lining with their right sides together and sew all around the outer edge. Turn and press.
5 Gather the crown to fit the brim. Place the gathered edge of the crown between the brim and the lining and, folding in the raw edge, sew the crown to the brim (Diagram clothes 6).

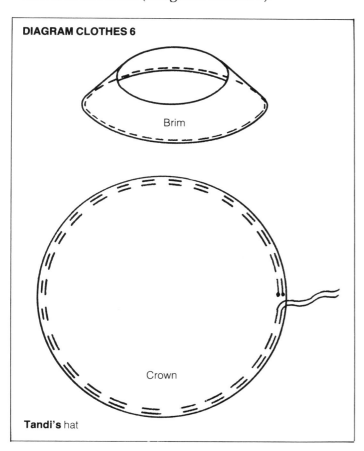

DIAGRAM CLOTHES 6

Brim

Crown

Tandi's hat

THE BABYGRO

Kimberley

Approximate lengths of the rib trim before folding.

1 piece 5 cm x 17 cm for the neck
2 pieces 5 cm x 10 cm for the sleeves

1 Sew the centre back seam **P** to **Q**. Sew the centre front seam **R** to **S**.

2 Place the back section and the front section together and sew the shoulder seams.
3 Fold back the front opening and put on the studs.
4 Gather the lower sleeves with rib trim. Sew the upper sleeves into the armholes.
5 Sew the sleeve seams and the side seams. Sew the inner leg (crotch).
6 Sew on the soles. These always look nicer if they match the rib trim (Diagram clothes 7).

THE PANTIES

Kirsten, Annabel, Jewel and Tandi

1 Sew the centre front and then the centre back seams.
2 Hem the waist to form a casing. Leave a little gap open.
3 Thread with elastic to fit the dolls' waists.
4 Sew the ends of the elastic together and sew the little opening closed.
5 Hem the lower legs and trim the very edge with lace.
6 Stretch and sew elastic to gather the lower legs.
7 Sew the inner leg (crotch) seam (Diagram clothes 8).

THE DUNGAREES

Frankie

1 Sew the centre front and then the centre back seams.
2 Hem the lower legs and sew the inner leg (crotch) seam.
3 Place the two sections of the bib with their right sides together, and hem on three sides, leaving the lower side open. Turn and press. Fold in the raw edge and top-sew the lower section closed.
4 Place the lower side of the bib, across the front of the dungarees right sides together, and sew into position.
5 Fold a narrow hem around the remaining top of the dungarees. Stretch and sew elastic to gather the top to fit the doll's waist.
6 Sew all around the straps, leaving the short straight side open. Turn to the right side with the aid of a small stick. Press. Make the buttonholes.
7 Fold in the raw edges on the straps and sew into position at the back of the dungarees. Sew the buttons to the bib.

THE JEANS

Simon

If possible try to find an old pair of jeans to use.

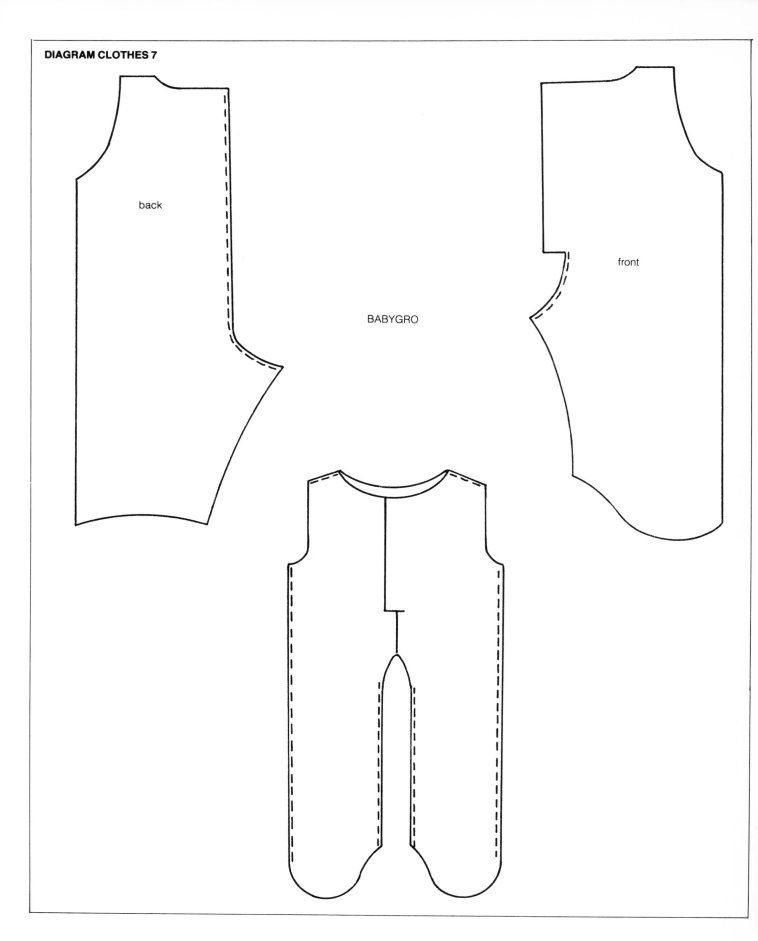

back

BABYGRO

front

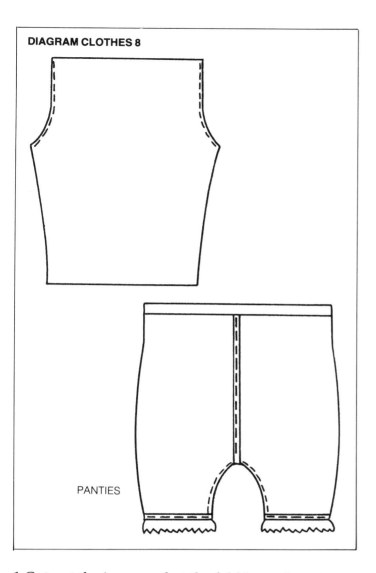

DIAGRAM CLOTHES 8

PANTIES

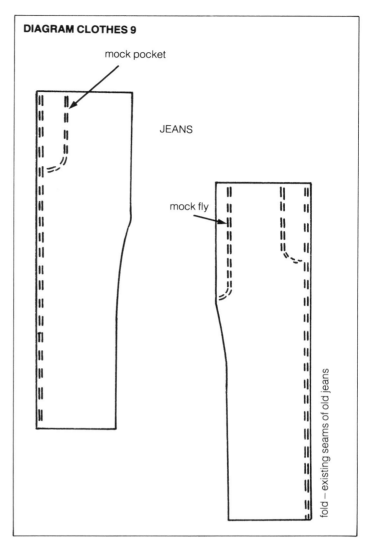

DIAGRAM CLOTHES 9

mock pocket

JEANS

mock fly

fold — existing seams of old jeans

1 Cut out the jeans so that the fold is on the existing double seams of the old jeans. Sew the centre back seam.

2 Using a contrasting thread, sew two rows of topstitching to form the mock pockets and on the left-hand side, the mock fly (Diagram clothes 9).

3 Sew the centre front seam for about two centimetres from the crotch to where the mock fly starts. Fold a narrow hem along the remainder of the front opening and insert a zip.

4 Cut a strip of 3 cm x 41 cm for the waistband. With right sides together, sew the waistband to the jeans, allowing about two centimetres to overlap on the left-hand side. Fold and hem by hand on the wrong side. Fold in the raw edges at either end of the band and topstitch. Make the buttonhole and sew on the button.

5 Using the belt loops from the old jeans, sew about five to the jeans.

6 Use household bleach and some cottonwool to fade the jeans at the pockets and the knees (Diagram clothes 9).

27

10 Shoes

Kirsten

1 Embroider the upper edge of the shoe and the entire strap, using a fancy machine-stitch. Make three bouillion roses on the front (optional).
2 Sew the back seam and sew on the sole.
3 Sew the strap to the inner side of the shoe. Feed the strap through the slits and tie to a small button or bead which is sewn to the outer side of the shoe.

Annabel

1 Sew the back seam and sew on the sole.
2 Thread ribbon through the slits and tie a bow.

Frankie

1 Fold contrasting bias binding in half and sew on the stripes.
2 Bind the entire upper edge of the tackie and the curved edge of the tongue, using the contrasting bias binding.
3 Sew the back seam and sew on the sole.
4 Tack the tongue into the front of the tackie on the wrong side.
5 Punch in four eyelets and thread with laces.

The socks for Kirsten, Frankie and Annabel were bought and are size 3 to 6 months.

11 Finishing touches and accessories

Well, how did you do? Now that you have completed your doll it is time to add those very important finishing touches.

Does your little boy need a few freckles? Dip a toothpick into light brown paint and dot a few freckles on the cheeks and above the nose.

Want to give a doll a pair of spectacles? Bend thin wire around coins (see sketch).

Make a catty using a Y-shaped twig, a rubber band and a small piece of felt or leather for the sling.

Buy a few accessories. The flowers in Kirsten's hair, her basket, Jewels beads and Frankie's straw hat are all readily available in departmental stores.

THE SILKWORMS

1 Cut out the mulberry leaf from green felt and embroider the veins in a contrasting green. Place in an empty cigarette box.
2 Roll a small piece of yellow nylon fur into a small ball for the cocoon and glue in the corner.
3 Cut a piece of white felt about 3 cm x 1,5 cm for each worm. Put glue on one side and roll up lengthwise. Wind thread around to form the sections. Sew two black beads and one red bead on to the "face" for the eyes and the mouth.

THE FISHING ROD

1 Use a piece of dowel stick about 55 cm long.
2 Bend four little pieces of wire to make the rod eyes and tie them to the stick with brightly coloured thread.
3 Bend a piece of wire to make a fish-hook and tie to one end of a piece of string about 60 cm long.
4 Thread the string through the rod eyes and secure the string at the top of the rod with glue or tape.

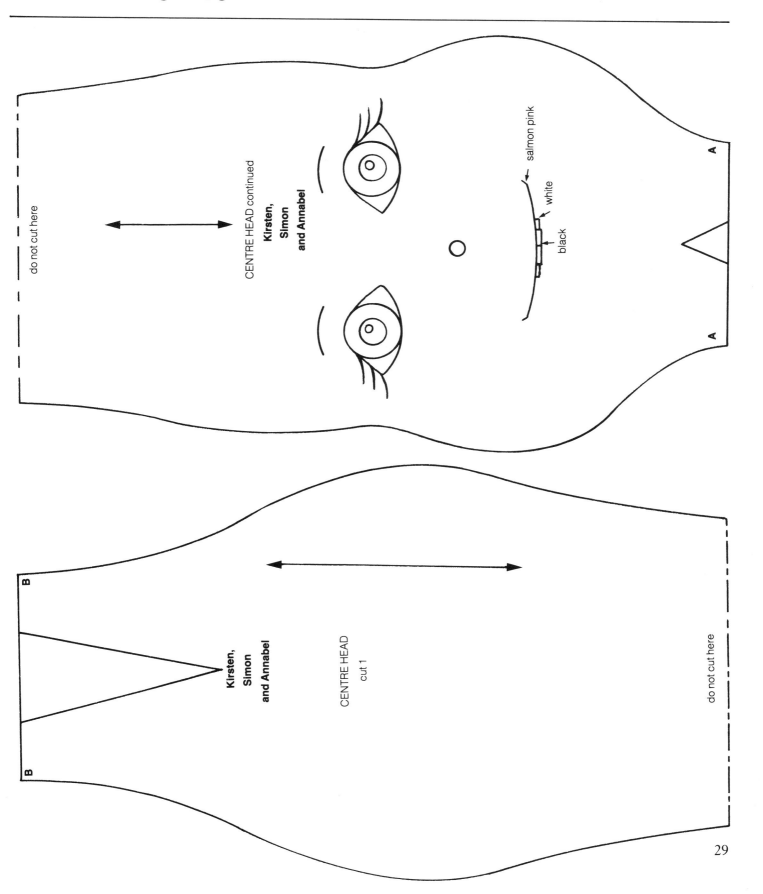

CENTRE HEAD continued

Kirsten, Simon and Annabel

do not cut here

salmon pink

white

black

A

A

B

B

Kirsten, Simon and Annabel

CENTRE HEAD

cut 1

do not cut here

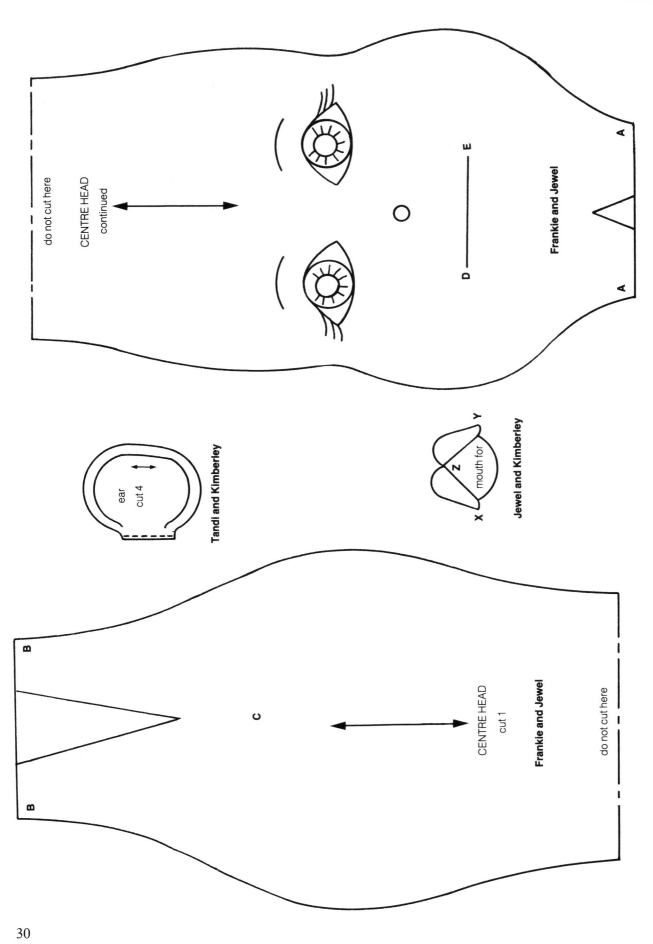

do not cut here

CENTRE HEAD
continued

E

D

Frankie and Jewel

A

A

Tandi and Kimberley

ear
cut 4

Y

Z

mouth for

X

Jewel and Kimberley

B

B

C

CENTRE HEAD
cut 1

Frankie and Jewel

do not cut here

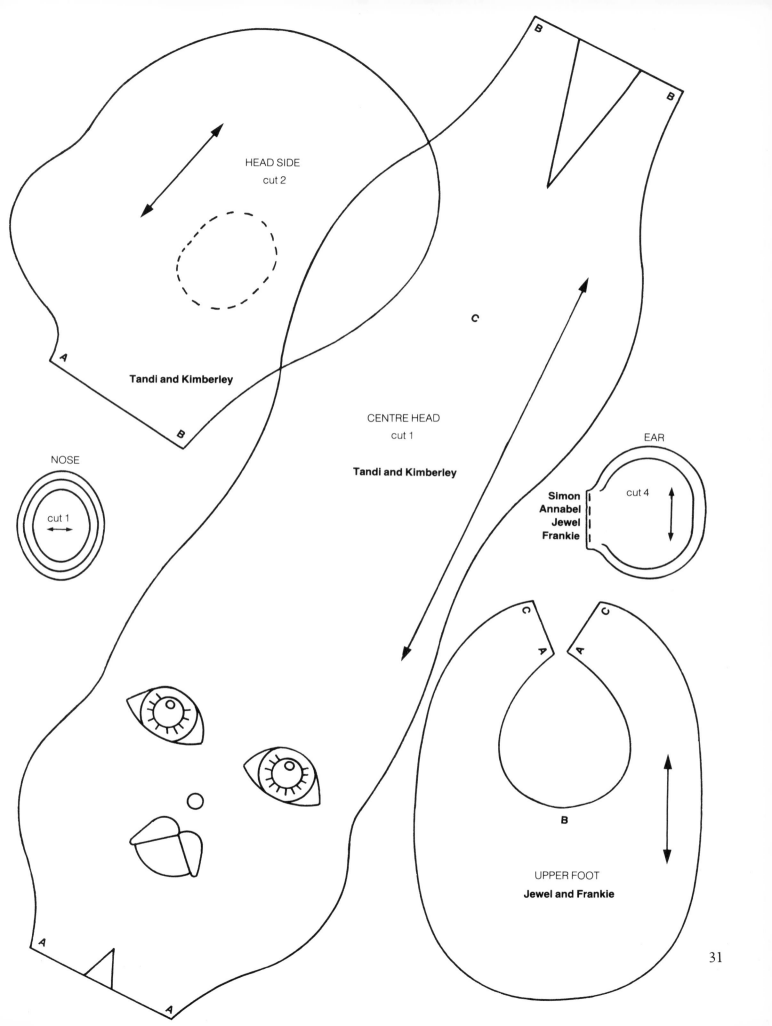

HEAD SIDE
cut 2

Tandi and Kimberley

NOSE

cut 1

CENTRE HEAD
cut 1

Tandi and Kimberley

EAR

cut 4

Simon
Annabel
Jewel
Frankie

UPPER FOOT

Jewel and Frankie

31

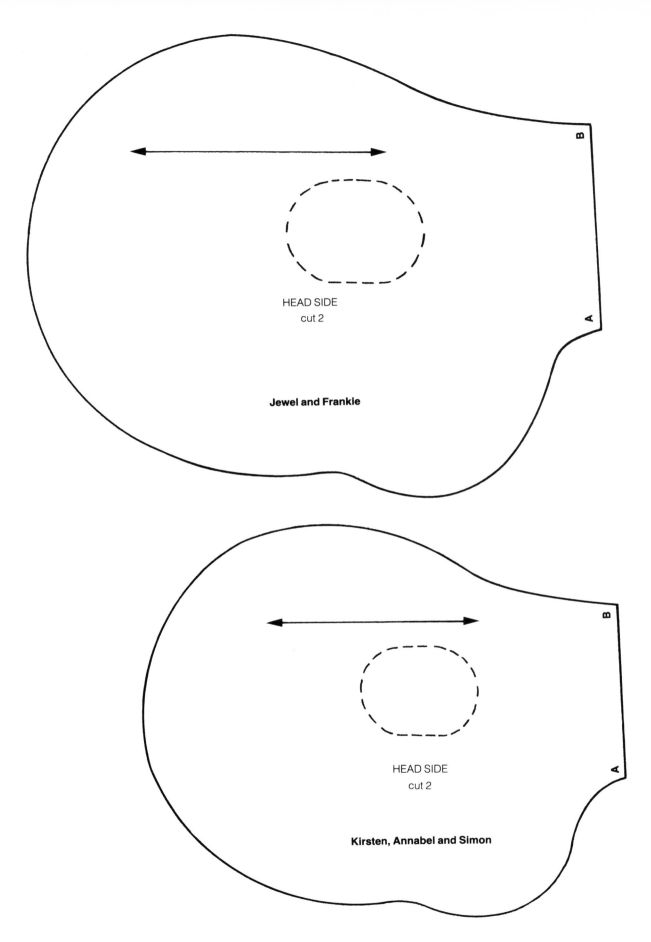

HEAD SIDE
cut 2

Jewel and Frankie

HEAD SIDE
cut 2

Kirsten, Annabel and Simon

32

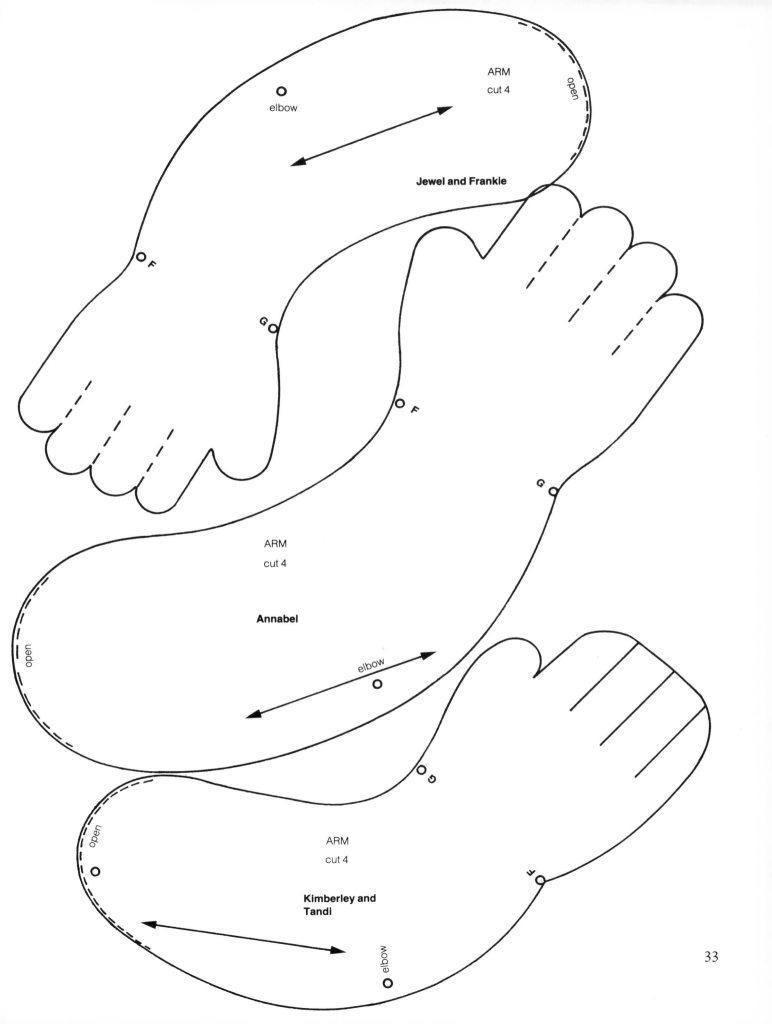

ARM
cut 4

Jewel and Frankie

elbow

open

F

G

F

G

ARM
cut 4

Annabel

open

elbow

G

open

ARM
cut 4

**Kimberley and
Tandi**

F

elbow

33

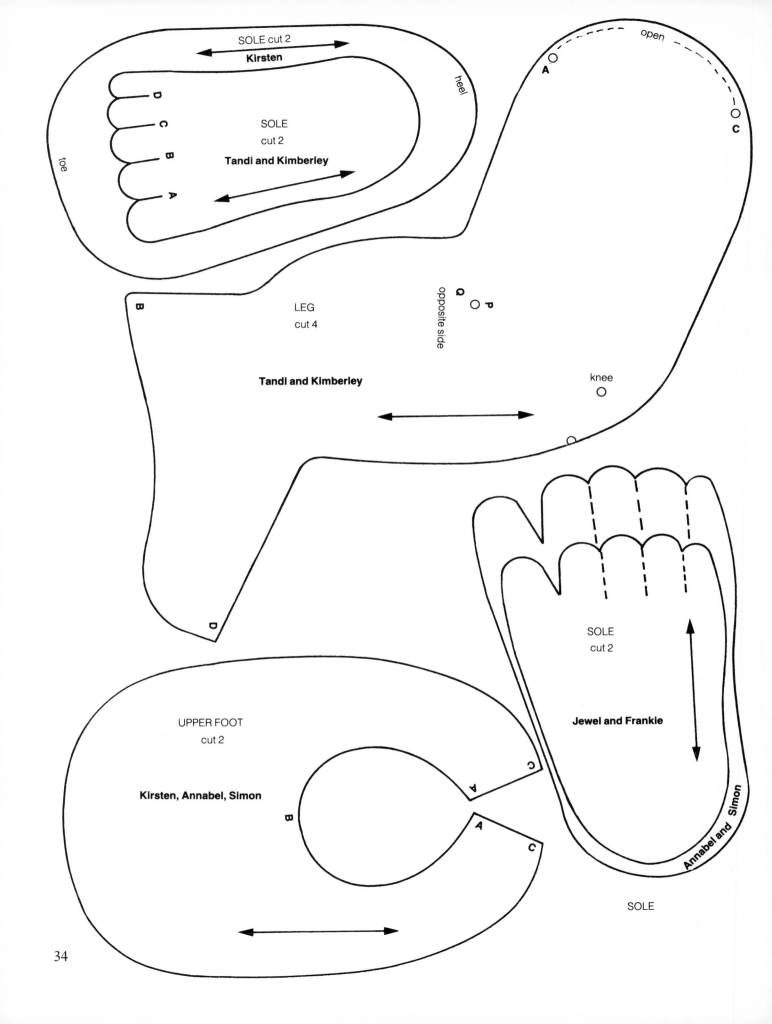

SOLE cut 2
Kirsten

SOLE
cut 2
Tandi and Kimberley

toe

heel

open

A

C

LEG
cut 4

Tandi and Kimberley

opposite side

Q

P

knee

B

D

SOLE
cut 2

Jewel and Frankie

UPPER FOOT
cut 2

Kirsten, Annabel, Simon

B

A

C

A

C

Annabel and Simon

SOLE

Kirsten

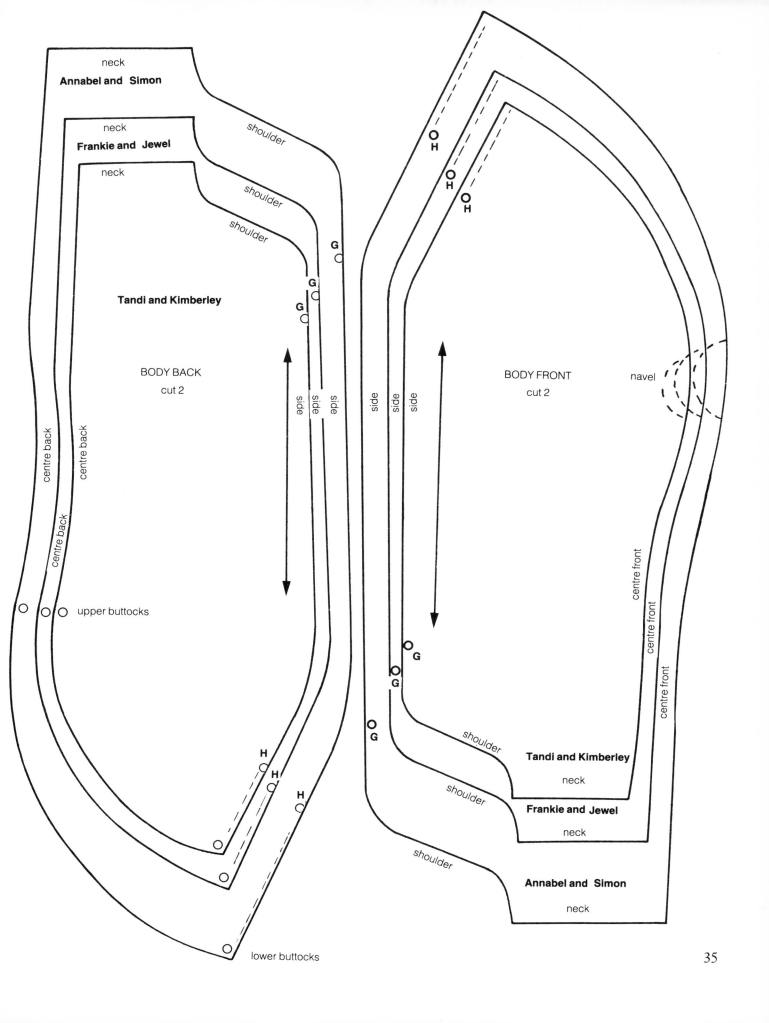

neck

Annabel and Simon

neck

Frankie and Jewel

neck

shoulder

shoulder

shoulder

Tandi and Kimberley

G

G

G

BODY BACK
cut 2

centre back

centre back

centre back

side
side
side

side
side
side

BODY FRONT
cut 2

navel

H
H
H

upper buttocks

centre front

centre front

centre front

G

G

G

shoulder

Tandi and Kimberley

neck

H

H

H

shoulder

Frankie and Jewel

neck

shoulder

Annabel and Simon

neck

lower buttocks

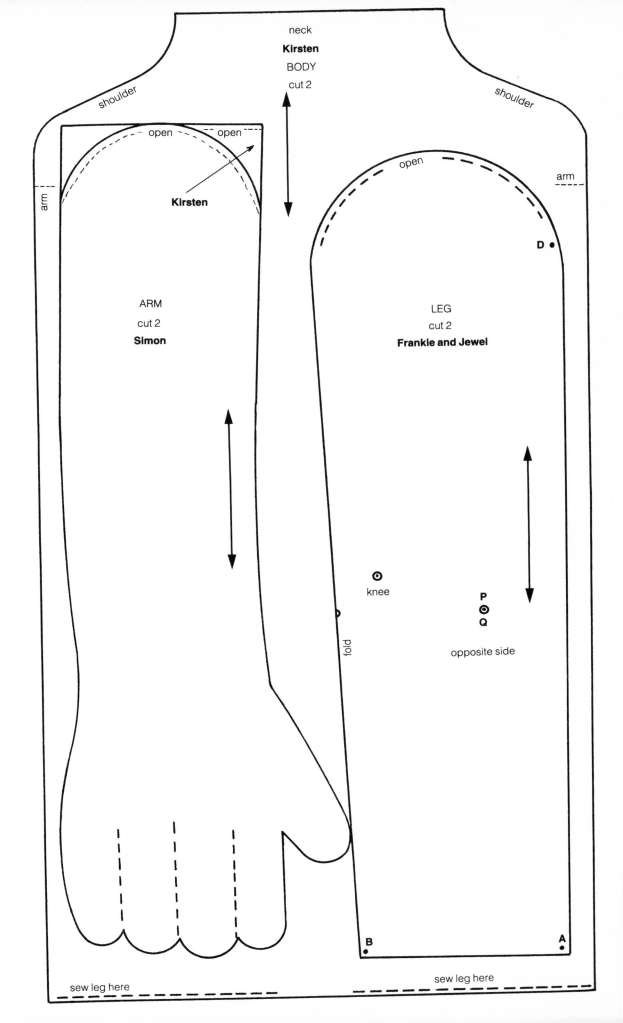

neck

Kirsten
BODY
cut 2

shoulder

shoulder

open   open

arm

open

arm

Kirsten

D •

ARM
cut 2
Simon

LEG
cut 2
Frankie and Jewel

knee ⊙

P
⊙
Q

fold

opposite side

B •

A •

sew leg here

sew leg here

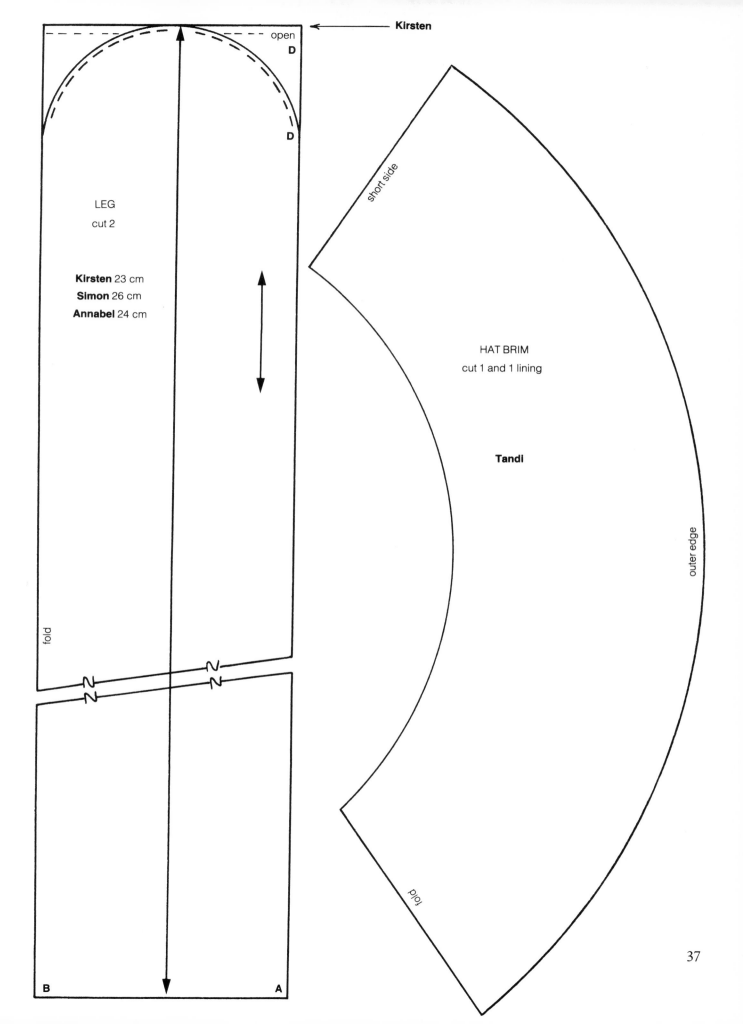

open

Kirsten ⟵

D

D

LEG

cut 2

Kirsten 23 cm
Simon 26 cm
Annabel 24 cm

fold

B   A

short side

HAT BRIM

cut 1 and 1 lining

Tandi

outer edge

fold

37

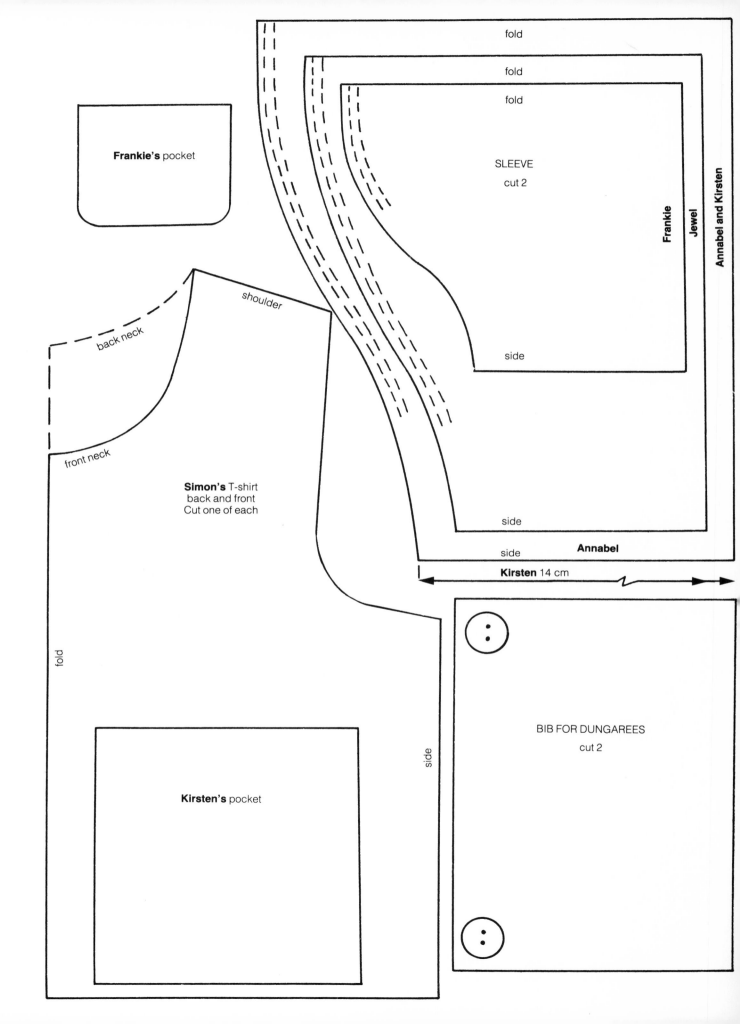

Frankie's pocket

fold

fold

fold

SLEEVE

cut 2

Frankie

Jewel

Annabel and Kirsten

side

side

side **Annabel**

Kirsten 14 cm

shoulder

back neck

front neck

Simon's T-shirt
back and front
Cut one of each

fold

side

Kirsten's pocket

BIB FOR DUNGAREES

cut 2

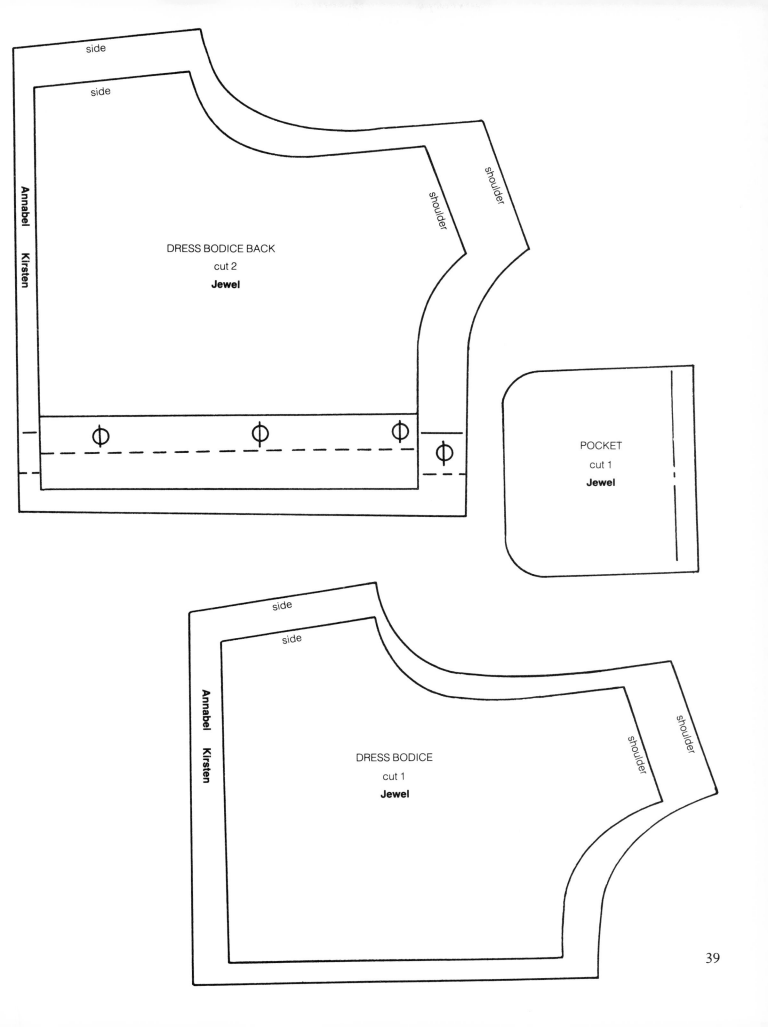

side

side

shoulder

shoulder

Annabel Kirsten

DRESS BODICE BACK

cut 2

Jewel

POCKET

cut 1

Jewel

side

side

shoulder

shoulder

Annabel Kirsten

DRESS BODICE

cut 1

Jewel

39

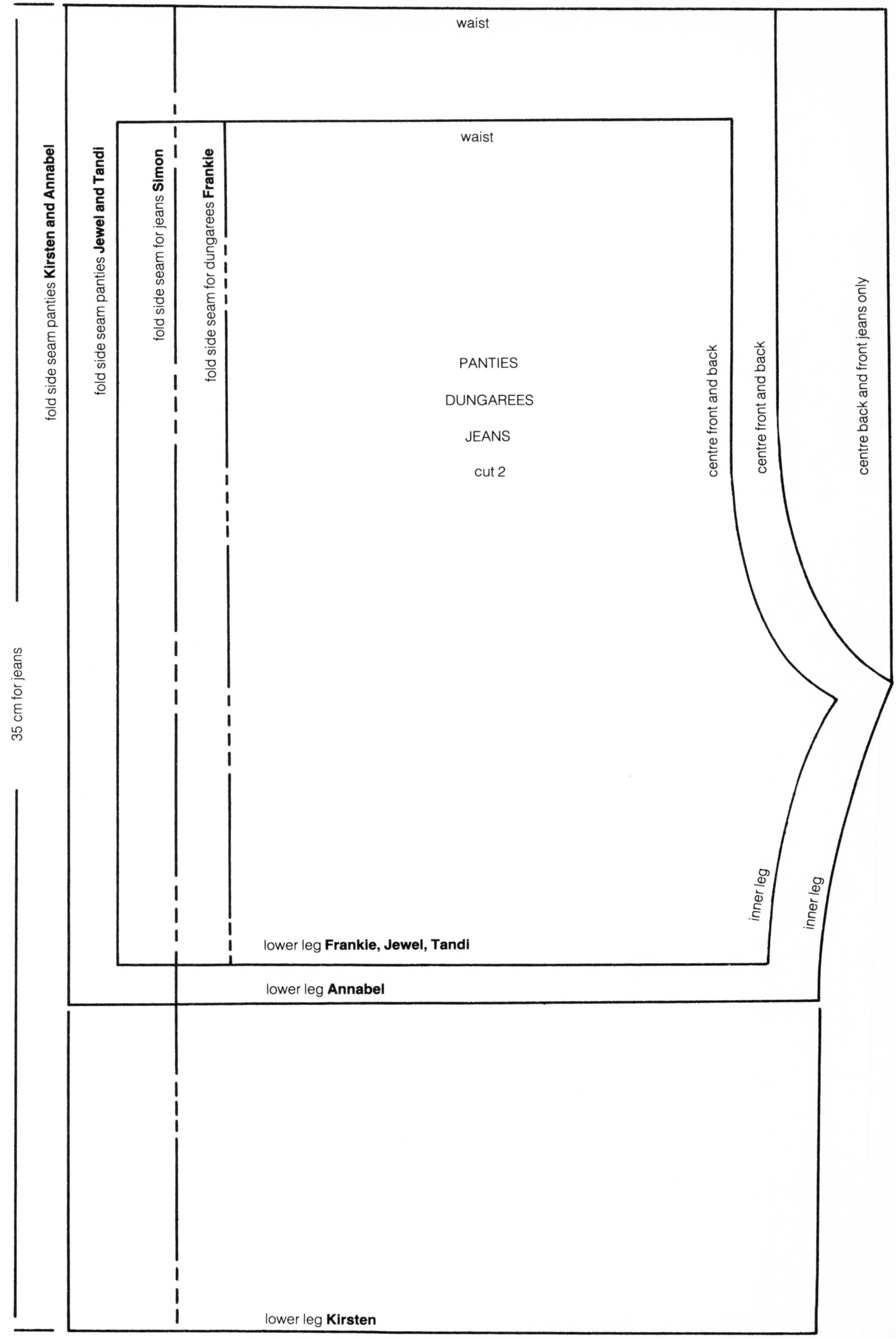

waist

waist

fold side seam panties **Kirsten and Annabel**

fold side seam panties **Jewel and Tandi**

fold side seam for jeans **Simon**

fold side seam for dungarees **Frankie**

centre front and back

centre front and back

centre back and front jeans only

PANTIES

DUNGAREES

JEANS

cut 2

35 cm for jeans

inner leg

inner leg

lower leg **Frankie, Jewel, Tandi**

lower leg **Annabel**

lower leg **Kirsten**

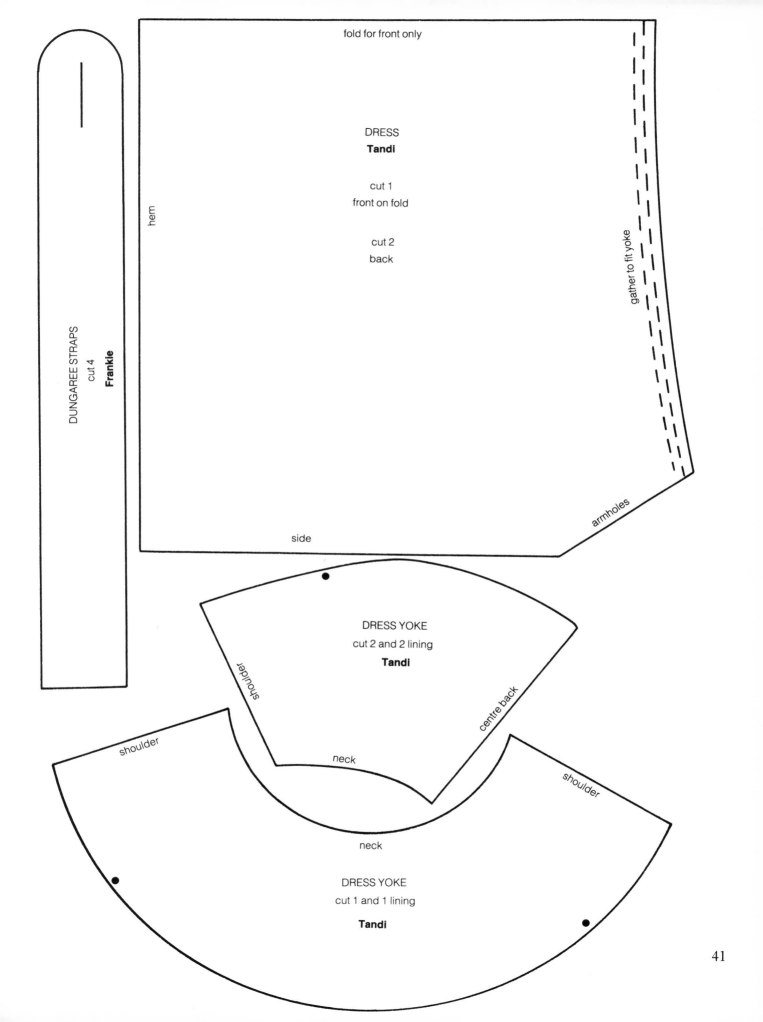

fold for front only

DRESS
Tandi

cut 1
front on fold

cut 2
back

hem

gather to fit yoke

side

armholes

DUNGAREE STRAPS
cut 4
Frankie

DRESS YOKE
cut 2 and 2 lining
Tandi

shoulder

neck

centre back

shoulder

shoulder

neck

neck

DRESS YOKE
cut 1 and 1 lining
Tandi

41

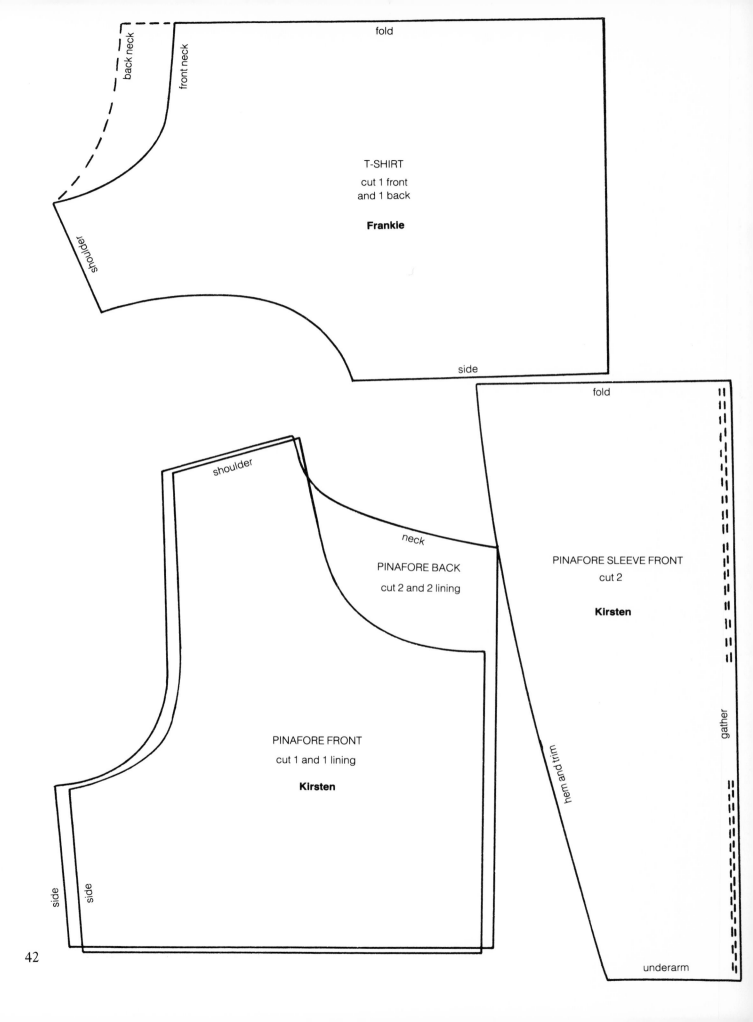

back neck

front neck

fold

shoulder

T-SHIRT

cut 1 front
and 1 back

Frankie

side

fold

shoulder

neck

PINAFORE BACK

cut 2 and 2 lining

PINAFORE SLEEVE FRONT

cut 2

Kirsten

gather

PINAFORE FRONT

cut 1 and 1 lining

Kirsten

hem and trim

side

side

underarm

42

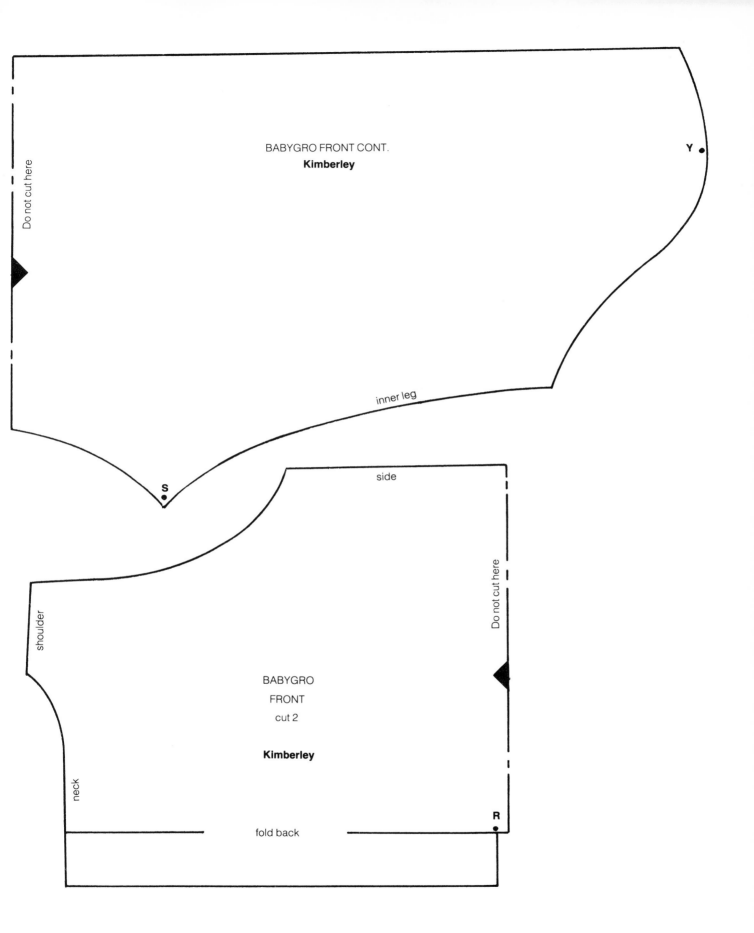

BABYGRO FRONT CONT.
Kimberley

Y

Do not cut here

inner leg

S

side

shoulder

Do not cut here

BABYGRO
FRONT
cut 2

Kimberley

neck

fold back

R

43

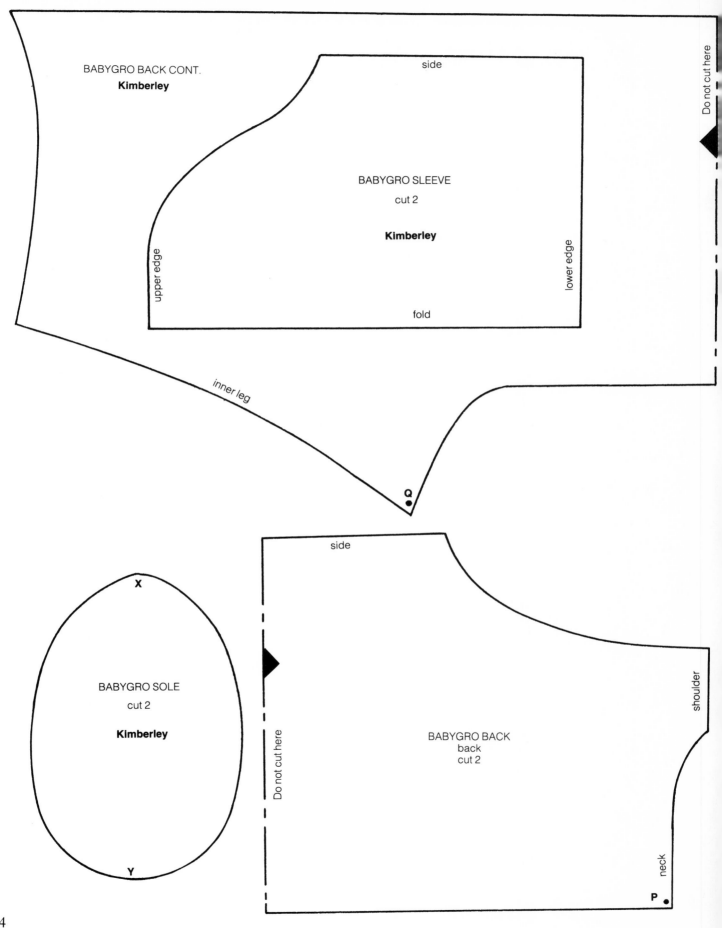

BABYGRO BACK CONT.
Kimberley

side

BABYGRO SLEEVE

cut 2

Kimberley

upper edge

lower edge

fold

inner leg

Do not cut here

Q

side

X

BABYGRO SOLE

cut 2

Kimberley

Y

Do not cut here

BABYGRO BACK
back
cut 2

shoulder

neck

P

44

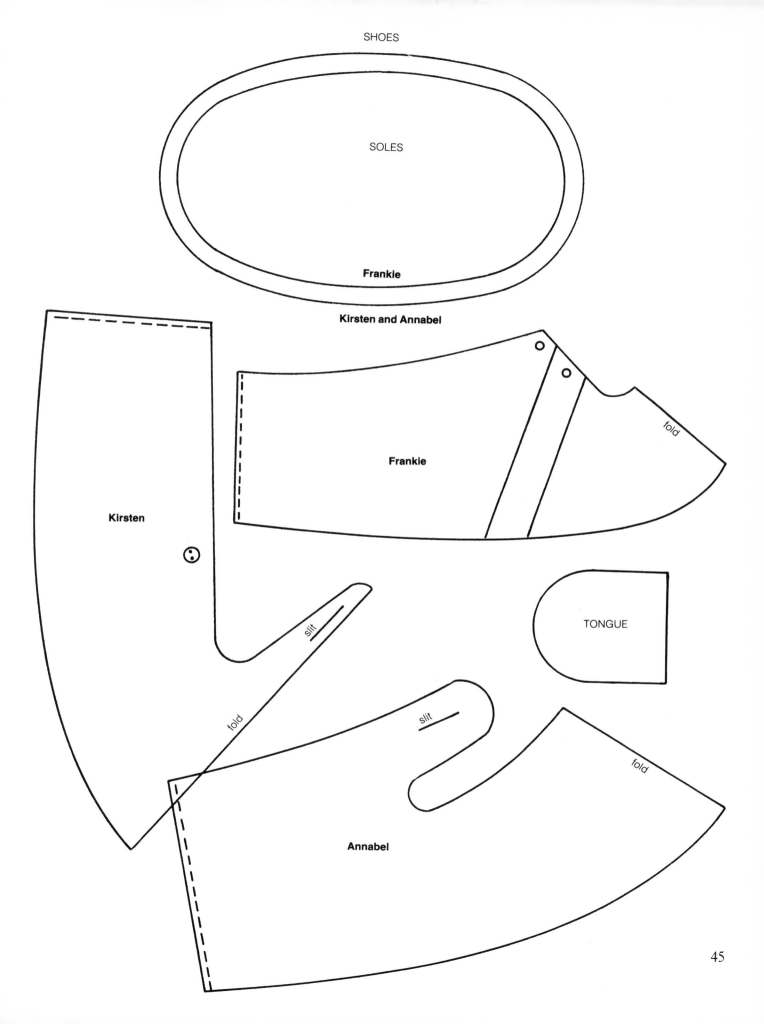

SHOES

SOLES

Frankie

Kirsten and Annabel

Kirsten

Frankie

TONGUE

slit

fold

fold

slit

fold

Annabel

45

Kirsten's   SHOE STRAP

MULBERRY   LEAF

Kimberley's

TEDDY

cut 2

SPECTACLES

THE DOLL STAND
The diagram for the doll stand is self-explanatory.

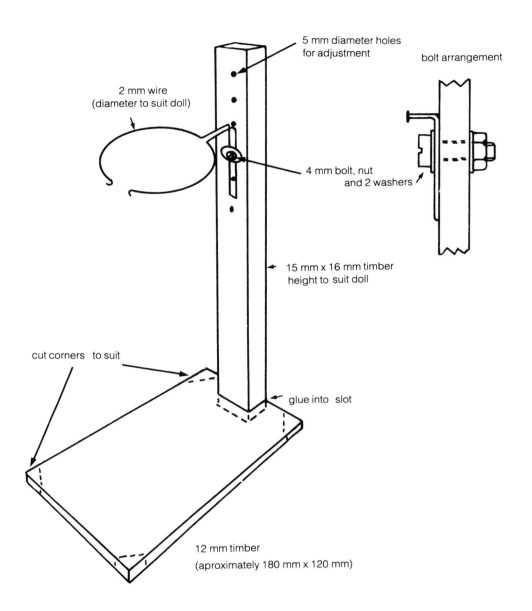

5 mm diameter holes
for adjustment

bolt arrangement

2 mm wire
(diameter to suit doll)

4 mm bolt, nut
and 2 washers

15 mm x 16 mm timber
height to suit doll

cut corners to suit

glue into slot

12 mm timber
(aproximately 180 mm x 120 mm)